Greenwich Village

A PHOTOGRAPHIC GUIDE

Greenwich Village

A PHOTOGRAPHIC GUIDE

by Edmund T. Delaney and Charles Lockwood

with photographs by George Roos

Third, Revised Edition

Dover Publications, Inc., New York

Frontispiece: Gay Street is a delightful nook of diminutive Federal and Greek Revival houses largely secluded from nearby Sixth Avenue and Christopher Street, which it joins. Its occupants have been varied; in the middle of the nineteenth century it was noted for its Scottish weavers and in the earlier part of this century it was a "mini-ghetto"—the only all-Black block in the neighborhood. The street also served as a setting for Ruth McKenney's *My Sister Eileen,* a light-hearted novel about bohemian life in the Village during the Thirties. McKenney actually lived at No. 14. The story was adapted for the Broadway stage and the movies and in the 1950s came to life again as the musical *Wonderful Town.* Mary McCarthy lived at No. 18 at a time when she "exulted in being poor and alone."

Credits for Photographs
Pages 5, 6, 7 (right), 14, 15, 16, 17, 24, 31 (bottom), 32, 33, 35, 36, 37, 39 (left), 40 (bottom), 41, 42, 43, 44 (bottom left and right), 45 (bottom), 46, 47, 48, 50 (top), 51 (bottom), 52, 53, 58, 62 (bottom), 65, 67 (bottom), 69 (right), 70, 77 (right), 78 (left), 81, 84 (bottom), 87, 89, 91 by Edmund V. Gillon, Jr.
Pages 25, 38, 75, 85 (top) by Blanche Cirker.
Pages 7 (left), 69 (left), courtesy of The New-York Historical Society, New York City.
Page 114 © Peter Cunningham. Courtesy C. J. Strauss & Company.
All other photographs are by George Roos.

Published in Canada by General Publishing Company, Ltd., 30 Lesmill Road, Don Mills, Toronto, Ontario.
Published in the United Kingdom by Constable and Company, Ltd., 10 Orange Street, London WC2H 7EG.

Greenwich Village: A Photographic Guide was first published by Dover Publications, Inc., in 1976. The third, revised edition was published in 1980.

International Standard Book Number: 0-486-23114-3
Library of Congress Catalog Card Number: 74-78593
Manufactured in the United States of America
Dover Publications, Inc.
180 Varick Street
New York, N.Y. 10014

Introduction

In the seventeenth and eighteenth centuries, New York was a small town clustered around the Battery. By 1800, New York's population was a mere 60,515, and the built-up area of the city only reached as far north as today's City Hall area. The rest of Manhattan was rolling country estates, rocky outcroppings, and forests punctuated by a few villages, mostly of Indian origin. One such country hamlet—called Sappokanican—stood at the site of Christopher Street. Nearby, Wouter Van Twiller, second Director-General of New Netherlands, owned a plantation of 200 acres known as Bossen Bouwerie.

In the early eighteenth century, the country estates and homes of such well-to-do families as the Bayards, Warrens, De Lanceys, Lispenards, and Van Cortlandts stood in the area by then known as "Greenwich." Another large landowner was Trinity Church, which had received a large grant from Queen Anne extending as far north as Sappokanican.

One of the most distinguished residences in the eighteenth-century city, "Richmond Hill," was built by Abraham Mortier in the 1760s on land leased from Trinity Church. This country home was Washington's headquarters for the summer of 1776, and he planned the Battle of Long Island there. When New York was the temporary capital of the new nation in 1789–90, Richmond Hill, the home of Vice President John Adams, was the scene of many receptions attended by prominent Americans and distinguished foreigners. In the mid-1780s, Aaron Burr, Vice President to John Adams, purchased Richmond Hill and he entertained there with his remarkable daughter Theodosia acting as his hostess at the tender age of fourteen.

By 1800, New York had crossed Canal Street in its ever-northward growth and approached what is now Greenwich Village. A road parallel to today's Greenwich Street led directly to the city further south. The country estates and farms of Greenwich were giving way to streets with measured lots, and small houses were built in groups of threes and fours. In 1797, Aaron Burr filed a still-surviving map, which divided his Richmond Hill estate into the standard 25- by 100-foot building lots and plotted today's Vandam, Charlton and King Streets.

By 1820, Greenwich Village's inevitable city growth had begun, but a natural disaster—the yellow fever epidemic of 1822—accelerated its development. In the eighteenth and early nineteenth centuries, public health standards in New York were on a nearly medieval level—garbage pails and chamber pots were emptied in the street, slaughter houses operated in the city, and burials frequently took place under the streets or in vacant lots. With these appalling conditions—and with ships coming into the harbor from all parts of the world—New York was plagued by regular epidemics of smallpox and yellow fever. During these epidemics, independently wealthy families left the city completely. Those who were tied to the city by business moved their families and establishments to Greenwich. According to a contemporary account, "Very few are left in the confined parts of town except the poorer classes and the negroes."

In 1822, for the first time, yellow fever appeared on the supposedly safe west side of town rather than in the run-down crowded streets along the East River. The city government declared the city below City Hall an "infected district'' and ordered all persons from their houses. Greenwich Village filled with a huge number of refugees overnight. Temporary wooden dwellings were quickly built for the displaced New Yorkers. With the onset of the first frost several months later, the yellow fever epidemic ended, and most of the refugees left Greenwich Village and returned to their former homes. But the area had become a part of the city, and the wooden dwellings, put up that summer for refugees, now housed laborers and immigrants.

The picturesquely skewed street pattern of the West Village—the blocks west of Sixth Avenue—is quite a contrast with the rectangular street layouts of Manhattan above 14th Street and is one of the Village's most distinctive features. Much of the Village escaped the often monotonous grid because its streets already had been laid out in a pattern, following old property lines, before the city selected the rectangular street pattern in 1811. Despite their lack of conformity with the 1811 grid plan, the city retained these existing jumbled streets which still delight New Yorkers.

In the 1820s, row-house construction swept into Greenwich Village. These Federal-style houses still stand on Charlton, King, and Vandam Streets and on Grove, Bedford, Commerce, and Christopher Streets. With a high basement, two stories, and pitched roof with dormer windows, they attracted middle-class families, often tradesmen working downtown or on nearby Sixth Avenue and craftsmen such as weavers and sailmakers working on the nearby Hudson River waterfront.

As it grew, Greenwich Village rapidly acquired urban shops and institutions. In the 1820s and 1830s, buildings with shops on the ground floor and family apartments on the upper floors rose along Sixth Avenue. Jefferson Market, built at the junction of Greenwich and Sixth Avenues in the 1830s, soon became a shopping hub for the area. Churches were also built in Greenwich Village; St. Luke's Chapel (1821) on Hudson Street and St. Joseph's Church (1833) on Sixth Avenue survive from that era.

While the West Village was a decidedly middle-class and working-class area in the nineteenth century, wealthy New Yorkers built palatial row houses in the 1820s and 1830s on the south, west, and north sides of Washington Square, just east of Sixth Avenue. In the seventeenth and eighteenth centuries, Washington Square was a marshland through which ran the Minetta Brook, a trout-filled stream that emptied into a swamp not far from Richmond Hill. After 1795, it was a paupers' burial ground and site of the city gallows. In 1826, the city converted it into the Washington Military Parade-Ground and a public park.

In the 1830s and 1840s, Washington Square and the surrounding area was home to wealthy and fashionable New Yorkers. Several blocks to the east and south, Bleecker and Bond Streets reputedly were the finest streets in the city—the setting for renowned Leroy Place and Depau Row terraces and row houses of unparalleled grandeur and opulence. Just east of Washington Square, fine mansions and the spectacular Colonnade Row graced verdant Lafayette Place. In the 1840s and 1850s, Fifth Avenue, which begins at Washington Square, became the favorite seat of fashion and soon was lined with mansions and row houses.

At the same time, three remarkable Gothic Revival churches rose north of Washington Square: the Church of the Ascension on Fifth Avenue at West 10th Street (1840–41), The First Presbyterian Church on Fifth Avenue between West 11th and West 12th Streets (1845), and Grace Church on Broadway at East 10th Street (1846). Handsome public buildings also opened in the area. A fine Gothic Revival building for New York University was built in 1837 on the east side of Washington Square and was demolished in 1894. The Astor Place Opera House (demolished) opened on Astor Place in 1847, followed in 1854 by the Astor Library on Lafayette Place, and by Cooper Union at Astor Place in 1859. In the 1840s, 1850s, and 1860s, those blocks of Broadway between Houston and 14th Streets were the location of the city's finest hotels, shops, clubs, and theaters.

From its earliest days, Greenwich Village has attracted writers, artists, and others of intellectual interests to its pleasant houses and streets. After his return from Europe, Thomas Paine, a rather controversial character and author of *Common Sense* and the *The Rights of Man*, lived in the Village until his death in 1809. William Dunlap, the painter and the recognized "Father of American Theater," lived in various houses in the Village. During his residence he wrote the first art history of the United States, *History of the Rise and Progress of the Arts of Design in the United States,* published in 1834 (Dover reprint, 1969).

Other notable writers living in or near Greenwich Village during the mid-nineteenth century were Washington Irving, James Fenimore Cooper, and Edgar Allan Poe. Poe wrote *The Fall of the House of Usher* while living on Sixth Avenue, near Waverly Place.

Artists were also well represented in Greenwich Village during this period. John Trumbull, known for his paintings of Revolutionary War scenes, lived for a time at No. 137 Waverly Place and spent his last years in the Village. In 1832, Samuel F. B. Morse was appointed Professor of Painting and Sculpture at fledgling New York University. At the school's Washington Square building he conducted the scientific experiments which culminated in the invention of the telegraph. Other artists in the Village included Erastus Field and George Inness, the landscapist, who had a studio next to Grace Church.

Because of all this literary and artistic activity, salons flourished in Greenwich Village, the best-known being that of Anne Lynch at No. 116 Waverly Place, near Washington Square. Frequent visitors to the Lynch home in the 1840s included Horace Greeley, William Cullen Bryant, Margaret Fuller, Bayard Taylor, and other leading writers and editors of the day. Poe himself was a frequent guest at these gatherings.

A less conventional group met at Pfaff's beer cellar at No. 653 Broadway, north of Bleecker Street. Rebelling against middle-class prudery and the increasing commercialization of life, this circle included Henry Clapp, the journalist; Fitz-James O'Brien, the poet; Thomas Bailey Aldrich, the editor; and two well-known actresses, Adah Isaacs Menken, who later became the mistress of Alexandre Dumas *père*, and Ada Clare, who enjoyed a similar relationship with Louis Gottschalk, the famous American composer and pianist. From time to time, Walt Whitman joined this group at Pfaff's.

By the 1860s, residential construction had largely ceased in Greenwich Village, and there was increasing commercial development in the area, particularly in its southern and eastern sections centering on Broadway. Since the late 1840s, Broadway, the site of the city's foremost hotels, stores, theaters, and concert halls, had also been the city's leading thoroughfare. In the early 1860s, A. T. Stewart opened his "uptown" store—then the largest department store in the city—at Broadway and East 10th Street, and the carriages of the city's wealthy "Upper Ten Thousand" jammed the nearby streets on shopping days. Fleischmann's Model Bakery, which stood next to Grace Church, was a coffee house patronized by the leading socialites, musical figures, artists, and writers of the time. On holidays and public celebrations, parades marched along dazzling Broadway into Union Square to be received by the city fathers.

But, in the 1860s and 1870s, the pressures of a growing city also brought about a decline in parts of Greenwich Village as well-to-do New Yorkers and businesses moved uptown. By the 1870s, the city's new houses were being built on Murray Hill and at the foot of Central Park. Greenwich Village was left behind by the city's growth, and the once proud houses came to be considered old-fashioned.

As old-timers died or moved away, their houses were taken over by immigrants who were flooding into New York. The Irish and Germans had established themselves in Greenwich Village by the Civil War. Thereafter, immigration into Greenwich Village was predominantly Italian. The streets south of Washington Square became one of the leading Italian neighborhoods in the city. Houses which had been built as fourteen-, sixteen-, or eighteen-room single-family residences in the 1820s and 1830s were broken up into rooming houses. An entire family, often joined by assorted relatives and even boarders, frequently occupied one cramped room. Over the years, especially between 1880 and 1900, many of the early nineteenth-century houses were torn down to make way for tenements and loft buildings. By the late nineteenth century, the area south of Washington Square was an appallingly overcrowded and impoverished neighborhood.

In the 1870s, the elegance of Broadway in the Greenwich Village vicinity evaporated as the Union Square and Madison Square areas to the north attracted the city's finest hotels and shops. The shops and old houses on or near Broadway gave way to warehouses and manufacturing lofts manned by cheap immigrant labor. Legislation governing working and living conditions was nonexistent; the dismal factories lacked adequate sanitary facilities or precautions against fire and accidents.

With the continuing growth of population, transportation created new problems. As the city spread north, the main arteries which united uptown with downtown became thoroughly congested with their horsecars, carriages and stages. By 1870, an elevated railroad along Greenwich Street had been completed to 30th Street and the original cable system was soon supplanted by locomotive power. By 1898 steam engines in turn were supplanted by electric power both on the Greenwich Street line and the Sixth Avenue line which had been built in 1876. Although elevated railroads improved transportation, they added to the blight of the neighborhoods through which they passed and the avenues on which the elevateds were built soon turned into dark and noisy eyesores. It was not until the mid-twentieth century that these monstrosities were finally removed.

Industry also lined the Hudson River waterfront in Greenwich Village. Washington Street had formerly marked the Hudson River's edge, but the waterfront had been filled in to West Street where railroad tracks were laid to carry freight down to the Hudson Terminal just below Canal Street. For several blocks off the waterfront, pleasant houses of the 1830s and 1840s were converted into stores and lofts or torn down to make way for factories, coal and lumber yards, or breweries.

Although tenements for immigrants and manufacturing lofts invaded the southern and eastern flanks of Greenwich Village in the late nineteenth and early twentieth centuries, lower Fifth Avenue and the blocks north of Washington Square remained a pleasant, well-to-do area of town houses and mansions. Full staffs maintained the great houses and, in this era of gracious living for the rich, the descendants of the old Knickerbocker families felt no temptation to leave the area and join the movement uptown.

An intellectual elite flourished in these orderly blocks north of Washington Square. Henry James, born at nearby No. 27 Washington Place, used this established life as a backdrop in *Washington Square*. For his description in the book, he relied on memories of his grandmother's house at No. 18 Washington Square North.

William Dean Howells, the editor and critic, lived in the Village after he came to New York from Boston and considered the benches in Washington Square his favorite spot. Howells saw much of his friend Mark Twain, who lived in a number of different houses along or near lower Fifth Avenue. Though not a part of the literary establishment of the era, Richard Harding Davis, Stephen Crane, and William Sidney Porter (better known as O. Henry) also made their homes in Greenwich Village.

In the late nineteenth century, the world of art and architecture was also well represented in Greenwich Village. John Taylor Johnston, the first president of the Metropolitan Museum of Art, lived in a white marble mansion at the southwest corner of 8th Street and Fifth Avenue. As early as 1860, he had converted a part of his stables around the corner of West 8th Street into an art gallery. Johnston's art gallery was the first in the city to which the general public was admitted, and its popularity encouraged several New Yorkers to found the Metropolitan Museum of Art, with Johnston as president, in 1870.

A studio building, designed by Richard Morris Hunt, at No. 51 West 10th Street, was the home at this time of some leading American artists and sculptors, among them Albert Bierstadt, Frederick E. Church, Winslow Homer, William Merritt Chase, John La Farge, Edward Lamson Henry, Augustus Saint-Gaudens, Frederick MacMonnies, and Daniel Chester French. Across the street from the Studio Building stood the Tile Club where these artists and sculptors and others formed one of the most important intellectual groups in the nation.

Other artists living in the Village in the late nineteenth century preferred a more isolated life —such as the reclusive mystical painter Albert Pinkham Ryder who lived for a while on West 4th and East 11th Streets.

At the turn of the century, a staggering amalgam of social and economic groups lived in Greenwich Village—the well-to-do on the north side of Washington Square and on 9th, 10th, 11th, and 12th Streets; the middle class in the West Village; and the poor immigrants south of Washington Square. To the east stretched grimy blocks of warehouses and lofts. William Dean Howells aptly pointed out the social gulf between these diverse groups in Greenwich Village when he contrasted the "old-fashioned American respectability which keeps the north side of the Square in vast mansions of red brick, and the international shabbiness which has invaded the southern border and broken it up into lodging houses, shops, beer gardens, and studios."

At this very time, Greenwich Village was on the threshold of sweeping physical and social changes. Despite the construction of elevated railroad lines in parts of the Village in the 1880s, the neighborhood was still fairly isolated from the rest of the city. Seventh Avenue did not extend below 14th Street until 1910, and Sixth Avenue had not yet been cut through below Carmine Street. This relative isolation and the skewed streets lined with early nineteenth-century town houses gave the Village a quieter and more individualistic atmosphere than could be found elsewhere in New York. The neighborhood had character and historic tradition; space was available and rents were low. Because of these factors, a whole new generation of writers, artists, social workers, reformers, and crusaders moved into Greenwich Village in droves in the early years of the twentieth century.

In the years before World War I, writers and reporters who settled in Greenwich Village included Willa Cather, Lincoln Steffens, Frank Norris, Theodore Dreiser, Ida Tarbell, Jack London, and Edwin Arlington Robinson. Many of this group lived in a rooming house at No. 61 Washington Square South which, because of the creativity of its residents, was called the "House of Genius." Some of these writers became known as "The Muckrakers" because of their exposure of the political and social corruption of the day. They also attacked the dismal living and working conditions which were all too prevalent in large American cities at the time.

Other Greenwich Village residents worked actively to remedy these social abuses. Foremost was Mary Kingsbury Simkhovich, the daughter of an old patrician family. In 1902, she established Greenwich House, which soon became a leading center for those interested in welfare work in the United States. While people at Greenwich House were performing their good offices, the movement for legislation to establish minimum safety standards in industrial enterprises at last gained momentum, spurred on by a tragic event in the Village. In 1911, a disastrous fire ravaged the Triangle Factory at No. 22 Washington Place East, just off Washington Square. Many young garment workers perished because of inadequate safety exits and the absence of elementary fire-prevention safeguards.

In these years, the avant-garde of the left in the United States was more or less concentrated in Greenwich Village and attacked the complacency of turn-of-the-century American society. Victorian morality was to be supplanted by "free love." Marxism in various forms was the ideal.

The Masses, founded in 1910 by Max Eastman, was the mouthpiece of the young radicals who were to be seen around the Liberal Club on Macdougal Street. *Seven Arts*, founded in 1916 by James Oppenheim and Waldo Frank, linked new movements in art and architecture to the political and social goals of the new society. Its contributors included the nation's intellectual elite at the time, among them Sherwood Anderson, Padraic Colum, Floyd Dell, Theodore Dreiser, John Dos Passos, Robert Frost, Walter Lippman, Eugene O'Neill, John Sloan, and Van Wyck Brooks.

At this time, ferment also swept the arts. The Village was the scene of many new departures in drama. The Washington Square Players, which later became the Theatre Guild, was organized in 1915. The Provincetown Players emerged shortly afterward and, with such players and playwrights as Eugene O'Neill, Miriam Hopkins, Edna St. Vincent Millay, Susan Glaspell and Bette Davis, soon became the center of experimental theater in New York.

A new group of painters known as "The Eight"—or less flatteringly, but more memorably, as the "Ashcan School"—challenged academic and traditional art concepts. Arthur B. Davies, William Glackens, Robert Henri, Ernest Lawson, George Luks, Maurice Prendergast, Everett Shinn, and John Sloan made up "The Eight," and their paintings, echoing the social message of their literary friends and other verbal contemporaries, reflected the good and bad aspects of life in those days.

Gertrude Vanderbilt Whitney, member of a distinguished New York family, encouraged and aided the artistic avant-garde in the city and herself remodeled a stable on Macdougal Alley as a studio for her sculpture work. Mrs. Whitney's interest in young artists led, in 1914, to the opening of a special gallery which was devoted to American art and eventually became the Whitney Museum of American Art. The Museum remained on West 8th Street until 1949 when it moved uptown, first to West 54th Street and then to its present striking building on upper Madison Avenue.

Literary salons continued to flourish in Greenwich Village, the best known during this period being Mabel Dodge's at No. 23 Fifth Avenue. Her salon not only attracted leading writers and artists of the day but also social activists and labor organizers. With such guests as "Big Bill" Haywood of the International Workers of the World and the well-known anarchist Emma Goldman, New Yorkers readily agreed with Lincoln Steffens that "all sorts of guests came to Mabel Dodge."

Physical and social changes continued to transform Greenwich Village. In the 1920s Sixth Avenue was cut through south of Carmine Street to Canal Street and became a major north–south route. Seventh Avenue had already been opened between 14th Street and the end of Varick Street at Houston Street and left an ugly gash in the once-secluded streets of the West Village. In the 1930s, the IND subway was opened beneath Sixth and Eighth Avenues and replaced the dilapidated elevated railroads that blighted stretches of the Village. At this time Greenwich Village lost whatever physical isolation it had enjoyed in the late nineteenth and early twentieth centuries.

The new accessibility, coupled with considerable notoriety about bohemian life, highlighted Greenwich Village as the most exciting and sophisticated part of the city in the 1920s. The Village was now a "must" for New Yorkers and tourists. Along with the new tourists came restaurants, coffee houses, nightclubs, and shops—art galleries, stores with eccentric clothing, book stores. Night spots such as Bruno's on Washington Square South and the San Remo and Minetta Tavern on Macdougal Street were particularly popular. Equally well-known were such restaurants as Enrico and Paglieri on West 11th Street and Mother Bertolotti's on West 4th Street. Less reputable, but a major part of Village nightlife during the Prohibition era, were the many speakeasies, such as Chumley's.

Greenwich Village also became a highly desirable neighborhood in which to live for those fleeing the "dullness" of uptown or the smothered life of The Bronx or Brooklyn. High-rise apartment buildings, with canopies and doormen, replaced many of the mid-nineteenth-century mansions and row houses on lower Fifth Avenue. The brownstones on the delightful side-streets were remodeled into studio apartments or demolished to make way for middle-class apartment houses. Young people moved into the run-down blocks of tenements south of Washington Square.

The Village's long-standing cultural traditions flourished in the 1920s and 1930s. Writers e. e. cummings, Ernest Hemingway, Freda Kirchwey, and Edmund Wilson were all part of the scene. The musical world included the young Leonard Bernstein and Aaron Copland. Among the painters were Hans Hofmann, Edward Hopper, Walt Kuhn, Reginald Marsh, and Marcel Duchamp. Sculptors included Jo Davidson, Gaston Lachaise, and William Zorach.

The years after World War I also saw a further expansion of the academic community in the Village. The New School for Social Research was established in 1919 and subsequently became one of New York's most fertile centers of learning. In 1931, the New School opened its building on West 12th Street, which was later expanded through to West 11th Street. The Little Red School House, which opened on Bleecker Street in 1932, has been a pioneer in progressive education on the elementary school level.

Dramatic physical and social change has continued to sweep Greenwich Village in recent years. During the 1950s and 1960s, high-rise, high-rent apartment buildings rose along Sixth Avenue, on 8th Street in the Sailor's Snug Harbor leasehold domain, on 14th Street, and in the lovely twisting streets of the West Village.

New York University's post-World War II expansion has also changed the face of the Village. The mammoth apartment buildings and barren plazas of Washington Square Village and University Village replaced the run-down but still vital mélange of tenements, lofts, and shops south and east of Washington Square. N.Y.U. buildings—ranging from the sham neocolonial Vanderbilt Law School to the sleazy style of the Holy Trinity Chapel for Roman Catholic students—have replaced the quaint row houses of the 1820s and 1830s along the south side of Washington Square.

Other physical changes in Greenwich Village have been less striking than the high-rise construction but equally important to the texture of the neighborhood. Thousands of run-down tenements and brownstones, for instance, have been renovated into high-rent apartments. In the past twenty years, furthermore, some Village shopping streets have abandoned their neighborhood service function to gain a citywide clientele. West 8th Street, between Fifth and Sixth Avenues, has lost many of its restaurants, bakeries, and shoe-repair shops, and today is known to young people throughout the city for its boutiques, "hip" shoe stores, and quickie food stands.

In these years of massive rebuilding and renovation, Greenwich Village remains a testing ground for ideas and behavior that will either fizzle out there or emerge uptown and throughout the nation a few years later. The "beat generation" of the 1950s has disappeared from Greenwich Village—its monuments being several pleasant coffee houses on Bleecker and Macdougal Streets. But, in the 1960s and 1970s, Greenwich Village has been the setting for mixed black and white marriages, the pervasive drug culture, the women's liberation and gay liberation movements.

Greenwich Village also remains a center of cultural activity in the city and nation. The pattern of theaters and galleries in Greenwich Village, however, runs against the current vogue of concentrating a city's cultural facilities in one monumental—and often oppressive—complex like Lincoln Center. Theaters, galleries, and educational institutions are scattered throughout the Village—in buildings of all sizes and ages—and touch the daily lives of local residents.

Since 1967, the New York Shakespeare Festival, under the direction of the dynamic Joseph Papp, has occupied the old Astor Library on Lafayette Street. Theaters have sprung up in garages, vacant storefronts, brownstones, even one-time movie theaters near the Bowery—among them the La Mama, Bouwerie Lane, Jean Cocteau, and New York Theater Ensemble.

Some recent developments in the Village are alarming and have caused many New Yorkers to lament that the Village is "going downhill" or "changing." Dilapidated welfare hotels have become temporary homes—often for a period stretching into years—for drug addicts, alcoholics, derelicts, and large families on welfare that have been burned out of or evicted from previous quarters and cannot find apartments at low rent. As previously noted, in the late 1960s and early 1970s, the long block of West 8th Street between Fifth and Sixth Avenues lost much of its charm and took on the tempo of Times Square. The smell of hamburgers, pizza and souvlaki—all overlaid with the odor of slightly rancid grease—wafts onto the sidewalks in front of the quickie food joints. In warm weather groups of young people parade up and down the brightly lit narrow sidewalks or aimlessly doze or stand against parked cars and buildings. The sidewalks around Sixth Avenue are "home base" now.

Many Village residents are disturbed because high rents are driving creative individuals with limited incomes from the area. The New Yorkers employed in the arts who maintain their residences in the Village tend to be those who are already well established—Leontyne Price, Susan Sontag, Robert Rauschenberg, John Lennon, and Yoko Ono—to name a few. So, though the semi-annual Washington Square sidewalk art show may still draw eager crowds, Greenwich Village has lost many of its painters and sculptors. In their search for cheap and ample living and studio space, artists have taken over former light manufacturing lofts in SoHo and the Bond Street area. When the city altered its zoning regulations to allow apartment-studio lofts in SoHo, uptown galleries, occasional shops, restaurants, and artists with their entourages flocked to the fine century-old cast-iron buildings that distinguish the neighborhood. Some New Yorkers have found the charm and vitality that formerly characterized Greenwich Village in such nearby renascent—and cheaper—areas as Chelsea and the East Village.

Although no single solution to the problem of this exodus from the Village has been found, some definite steps have been taken. The J. M. Kaplan Fund sponsored the renovation of the former Bell Telephone Laboratories' building on West Street into studios and apartments for artists at moderate-income rents. After considerable delay and alteration of the original plans, an urban renewal project in the Greenwich and Washington Streets area, adhering to the precepts of Jane Jacobs by retaining a neighborhood feeling and avoiding the social dislocation that is usually associated with large developments, features apartment buildings of five and six stories for middle-income individuals and families, although not necessarily for artists.

The welfare hotels and honky-tonks have not appreciably lessened the Village's social and economic heterogeneity, cultural activity, or overall dynamism. Of course the Village is changing—as any city area must do in order to remain alive and vibrant, and especially an area like the Village, which initiates and tests new social and intellectual currents.

Despite social upheaval and extensive rebuilding and expansion, Greenwich Village still entrances New Yorkers with familiar scenes and events. The late afternoon sun strikes Washington Square Arch and the red-brick mansions along the Row. Enticing aromas waft out of the Italian bakeries and coffee houses along Bleecker Street. Small shops and intimate restaurants lie in wait along the twisting streets of the West Village. Hordes of shoppers surge in and out of the bazaar-like discount shops along 14th Street. The brownstones of West 10th and 11th Streets and the luxury apartment buildings of lower Fifth Avenue radiate prosperity and respectability. Excited crowds pack the streets for the Feast of St. Anthony.

These well-known images focus attention on Greenwich Village's finest quality—diversity.

The Village is a strikingly successful mélange of rich and poor, various ethnic groups and races, a spectrum of all ages, single people (including a large homosexual community) and families. The physical texture of the Village shows a remarkable variety for New York—noisy traffic-packed avenues and winding tree-lined streets and mews, shops and garages on otherwise residential streets, and modern high-rise apartment buildings and old row houses. It is possible for a Villager to spend all of his time within the boundaries of the Village—he can work, live, market, shop and amuse himself without leaving it.

Greenwich Village, with its continuing desirability as a place in which to live, runs counter to two powerful currents of contemporary American life—the homogenization of thought, food, dress and speech, and the segregation of Americans into antiseptic areas on the basis of race, age, and income. The Village still continues to be a place to seek out, face, and profit from the rich variety and vitality of America.

The businesses—restaurants, boutiques, shops, etc.—included in this book were chosen because they are typical of the Village. Inclusion or exclusion of any commercial enterprise should not be construed as a judgment of quality by the publisher.

The Village Voice Map of Greenwich Village.
Copyright © 1973 by The Village Voice.

Greenwich Village

A PHOTOGRAPHIC GUIDE

A view of the famous Washington Arch [1], Washington Square Park and
the apartment buildings on lower Fifth Avenue taken from New York
University's Loeb Student Center. The Empire State Building—a mile and
a half north at Fifth Avenue and 34th Street—rises in the background. To
the right is No. 1 Fifth Avenue, the first high-rise to be erected in the
neighborhood (1926). Poet Sara Teasdale committed suicide there in 1933.
The row on Washington Square North just to the left of the arch is actually
a wing of No. 2 Fifth Avenue, the apartment building that towers behind
it. The wing, erected as a concession to concerned New Yorkers who
protested the prospect of a high-rise building directly on the Square,
stands on the site of five homes built between 1835 and 1852, two of
which belonged to the Rhinelander family. Another of these houses, No.
18, had been the home of Elizabeth Walsh, grandmother of Henry James,
who used the house as the setting for his novel *Washington Square* (later
dramatized as *The Heiress*). Of the Square and the house, James writes:

> *The ideal of quiet and genteel retirement, in 1835, was found in Wash-
> ington Square, where the Doctor built himself a handsome, modern, wide-
> fronted house, with a big balcony before the drawing-room windows, and
> a flight of white marble steps ascending to a portal which was also faced
> with white marble. This structure, and many of its neighbors, which it
> exactly resembled, were supposed, forty years ago, to embody the last
> results of architectural science, and they remain to this day very solid and
> honorable dwellings. . . This portion of New York appears to many per-
> sons the most delectable. It has a kind of established repose which is not
> of frequent occurrence in other quarters of the long, shrill city . . .*

Washington Arch, standing at the middle of the northern edge of Washington Square Park, forms the focal point of views looking down Fifth Avenue. In 1889 Stanford White designed a temporary arch of wood and staff to commemorate the centenary of Washington's inauguration as President. It spanned Fifth Avenue near 8th Street. The handsome neoclassical arch proved so popular that it was decided to erect a permanent one and the present arch, also by White, was dedicated in 1895. Complementary statues of Washington adorn its northern facade: "Washington in War" (1916) [opposite left] by Hermon A. MacNeil and "Washington in Peace" (1918) [opposite right] by A. Stirling Calder—the father of Alexander. The bas reliefs are by the prolific Frederick MacMonnies. Both Calder and MacMonnies were closely associated with the 10th Street Studio which stood nearby and played an important role in the city's artistic life during the last half of the nineteenth century.

Washington Square Park is a people-watchers' paradise that attracts the young from all over the metropolitan area. When the weather is good it is filled with a mob listening to impromptu performers and soapbox orators.

3

A view of Washington Square taken from No. 2 Fifth Avenue shows the buildings that line Washington Square South: (from left to right) the monolithic Bobst Library (opened in 1972 and criticized for its complete lack of harmony with the Square), the Loeb Student Center, Holy Trinity Chapel, and Judson Memorial Church. Directly behind the Bobst Library can be seen the Washington Square Village (1958), now dwarfed by the more recent University Towers. The twin towers of the World Trade Center loom farther downtown. Originally marshland, the park has served New Yorkers as a potter's field, as a site for public hangings, and as a parade ground. In the late 1960s it underwent extensive renovation to increase its usefulness to the public.

New York University's original building [right top]—a handsome Gothic Revival structure considered a likeness of King's College Chapel in Cambridge, England—rose on the east side of Washington Square in 1837. In 1839, while a professor of chemistry and physiology at the university, John W. Draper developed what was probably the first photographic portrait of the human face. Samuel F. B. Morse worked on the telegraph while teaching painting and sculpture there—he was a distinguished painter in his own right. In 1894 the charming building was replaced by the present businesslike structure [2; opposite]. In *The American Scene,* Henry James lamented the destruction of the old building:

The grey and more or less hallowed University building—wasn't it somehow with a desperate bravery, both castellated and gabled?—has vanished from the earth, and vanished with it the two or three adjacent houses, of which my birth place was one.

Opened in 1965 at No. 251 Mercer Street, Warren Weaver Hall [2A; right bottom] houses the Courant Institute of Mathematical Sciences, which serves as N.Y.U.'s graduate department of mathematics and computer science. The Institute has done pioneer work in the theory and numerical solution of partial differential equations and specializes in research in probability, magneto-hydrodynamics, mathematical biology, computer science and electromagnetics. The award-winning building, with its bronze-toned glass and brick, was designed by Warner, Burns, Toan & Lunde to harmonize with the buildings already standing in the neighborhood.

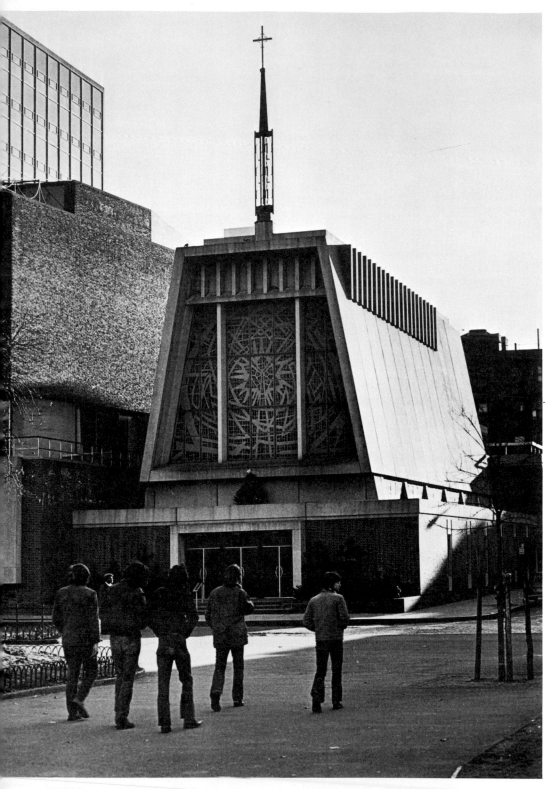

New York University's expansion in recent years has upset many New Yorkers. Rightly or wrongly, Greenwich Village residents charge that banal university buildings, such as the Holy Trinity Chapel [3; left] for the university's Catholic students and Loeb Center left of it, have destroyed the original scale of the square as a park surrounded by buildings of uniform height. The Loeb Center, used for student and faculty events, stands on the site of a rooming house at 61 Washington Square South; originally a mansion, it became known as the "House of Genius" because its lodgers included Willa Cather, O. Henry and Theodore Dreiser.

The Judson Memorial Church [4; opposite], built by McKim, Mead and White in 1892 in a masterful demonstration of the Italian Renaissance Eclectic style, has been known in recent years for its folk music, jazz and avant-garde theatricals. The church was named after the Baptist missionary Adoniram Judson; the cornerstone contains a copy of his translation of the Bible into Burmese. The stained-glass windows are by John La Farge and the marble relief on the south wall of the chancel was executed by Herbert Adams after plans by Augustus Saint-Gaudens. The church's tower, which recalls a Roman campanile, was at one time the home of the poet Edwin Arlington Robinson, and recently has been used by N.Y.U. for women's dormitory space. With its robust scale and yellow-brick facade, the church contrasts startlingly with the Holy Trinity Chapel to the east.

During the Washington Square Outdoor Art Exhibit, which radiates 80 blocks around the Square, about 1000 ardent amateurs and seasoned professionals, representing as many different schools of art as levels of competence and using media ranging from oil on canvas to lucite, display their work side by side. It is not unusual to see a viewer and an artist in heated argument over the fine points of esthetics. The semiannual show has been a Village attraction since 1933. This view [above] is of Thompson Street, with Judson Memorial Church on the left and Holy Trinity Chapel on the right. In the background beyond the arch rise two apartment houses at the foot of Fifth Avenue.

The imposing Greek Revival houses of the 1830s along the north side of Washington Square [opposite], east of Fifth Avenue, are some of the finest remaining nineteenth-century structures in New York. Long known collectively and simply as "The Row," they are seen to great advantage when the afternoon sun brightens the red-brick facades punctuated by white marble entrances. Although the fronts of most of the houses have been little changed, the interiors have been altered into offices for New York University and into fine apartments.

In 1884, No. 3 Washington Square North [5; opposite]—the only house in "The Row" with an altered facade—was remodeled from a one-family residence into fashionable apartments, known as the "Studio Building" (not to be confused with the "Studio Building" that stood on 10th Street and was also a part of New York's artistic world). In the twentieth century No. 3 was the home of such well-known painters as William Glackens, Rockwell Kent, Ernest Lawson, Guy Pène duBois and Walter Pach. Edward Hopper, one of the greatest American painters, lived and painted in the building for many years, dying there in 1966.

The handsome town houses bordering the north side of the square evoke visions of a more tranquil and beautiful New York in the late nineteenth and early twentieth centuries. In addition, many of them claim strong ties with the literary heritage of America, particularly with the work of Henry James and Edith Wharton. Miss Wharton, the author of *Ethan Frome* and *The Age of Innocence,* lived at No. 7 Washington Square North [6; right] in 1881.

Two famous authors have lived just off the Square in the Beaux-Arts apartment house at No. 82 Washington Place [7; above left]: the novelist Willa Cather, who spent much of her creative life in the Village, and Richard Wright, whose *Native Son* has become a classic of Black literature.

In 1909 Edwin Arlington Robinson, three-time Pulitzer-prize-winner for poetry, lived in a small cottage behind the handsome house at 121 Washington Place [8; above right].

In the nineteenth century, Macdougal Alley [opposite], off Macdougal Street, was lined with the stables of the homes on Washington Square North. In the 1920s and 1930s, the stables were remodeled into studios and apartments. Today the small-scaled, picturesque buildings and the quiet of this street are a pleasant contrast to the imposing houses on the Square to the south, hectic 8th Street one short block to the north, and the high-rise apartments along Fifth Avenue to the east. The atmospheric gas lamps in the alley, frequently pointed out as the last surviving from nineteenth-century New York, are actually modern additions. Among the artists who lived or worked in Macdougal Alley were Ernest Lawson and Jo Davidson. Gertrude Vanderbilt Whitney originally held her Studio Club in the alley before moving it to 8th Street.

Washington Mews [above], paved with Belgian blocks, runs between Fifth Avenue and University Place in back of Nos. 1–13 Washington Square North. The buildings along the north side of the mews were originally stables. This row of diminutive houses on the south side was built in the 1930s on the site of the deep gardens of the Washington Square North houses. Mary Emmett, who lived at No. 54, was a friend of Sherwood Anderson.

To many New Yorkers and tourists, 8th Street between Broadway and Sixth Avenue [opposite] epitomizes the Village. Bookshops and restaurants share the street with boutiques, record shops, and stand-up quick-food joints. Many Villagers regard the street as a tawdry eyesore; its development as the only principally commercial thoroughfare among the sidestreets off Fifth Avenue stems from the outgrowth of business from the old Jefferson Market in the Village Square. Busy shoppers rarely look above the gaudy store fronts to notice the nineteenth-century facades of many of the buildings. Many notable people have lived on the street: Charles Dana, a pioneer of modern news editing, at No. 24; painter Hans Hofmann at Nos. 52–54; sculptor Gaston Lachaise at No. 55. James Fraser (creator of the Indian head nickel) and his wife were living at No. 28 when they put up Edwin Arlington Robinson while he wrote *Tristram*.

17

In 1931, Gertrude Vanderbilt Whitney moved her Studio Club from Macdougal Alley to the building at No. 8 West 8th Street [9; opposite left], renaming the collection the Whitney Museum of American Art. The museum flourished here until 1949, when it moved to West 54th Street. It is now housed in a new building on Madison Avenue and 75th Street, where it continues to play an active role in the nation's cultural life. The old 8th Street building carries on its artistic associations as the New York Studio School of Drawing, Painting and Sculpture.

The Greek Revival house at No. 10 West 9th Street [10; opposite right] was built in 1841 for lumber merchant Thomas McKie. The studio on top, receiving the north light so desired by artists, was a later addition. William Glackens, a painter and member of "The Eight" or "Ashcan School" which revolutionized American painting in the early years of the century, lived in the house during the period between the two world wars.

"The Portsmouth" at Nos. 38–44 West 9th Street [11; right] is a fine six-story apartment house designed by Ralph Townsend and built in 1882. The terra-cotta panels and brickwork, typical of the Queen Anne style that flourished in New York from 1880 to 1893, are exceptionally handsome. "The Portsmouth" and its similar neighbor, "The Hampshire" (also by Townsend, but built a year later) at Nos. 46–50, fit harmoniously into this block of town houses and apartment buildings. Famous residents of "The Portsmouth" have included Ida Tarbell, the muckraking journalist and historian, and the painter Hans Hofmann.

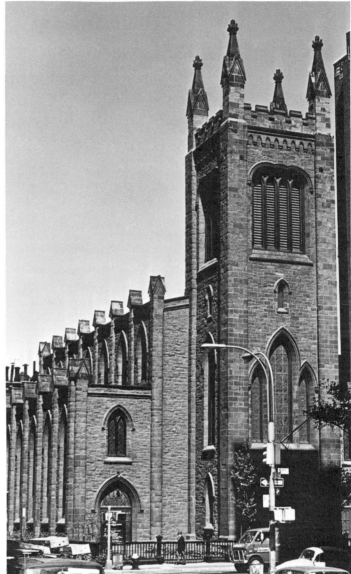

The former Lockwood de Forest residence [12; above left], built at No. 7 East 10th Street by Van Campen Taylor in 1887, is probably the only town house in New York with an East Indian influence. The teakwood of the elaborately carved bay window and in the trim around the door is better preserved than the brownstone of neighboring buildings. A room from a Jain temple was donated to the Metropolitan Museum by de Forest and his brother Robert, a museum trustee and president.

The Church of the Ascension (Episcopal) [13; above right], built 1840–41 at 10th Street, was one of the major buildings to be erected on this portion of Fifth Avenue. Designed by Richard Upjohn, architect of Trinity Church downtown, it exemplifies

the many fine Gothic Revival brownstone churches erected in New York in the mid-nineteenth century. In 1844 the church was the scene of the wedding of President John Tyler and Julia Gardiner, who lived nearby at Colonnade Row.

The interior of the Church of the Ascension [opposite] was redecorated by the prestigious New York architectural firm of McKim, Mead and White in the 1880s. Augustus Saint-Gaudens executed the marble altar relief. John La Farge did the great altar mural, representing *The Ascension of Our Lord,* as well as many of the stained-glass windows. The opalescent glass in these windows, the result of experiments La Farge conducted with Louis Tiffany, is irreplaceable.

The impressive scale and elaborate brownstone carving of Nos. 14–16 West 10th Street [14; opposite] epitomize the prevalent taste of the 1850s, when the houses were built. In 1900–01 No. 14 was inhabited by Mark Twain, and it is said that he moved because his wife had difficulty in running the large house. Today some people claim the house is haunted by the ghosts of previous occupants.

West 10th Street [above] between Fifth and Sixth Avenues is one of the most delightful blocks in the city—a mixture of trees, sun and well-maintained row houses dating from the late 1850s to the early 1930s. The Anglo-Italianate style brownstone fronts at Nos. 20–38 constitute the "English Terrace" (1855–56, attributed to James Renwick, Jr.), and recall the wealth and pomp of New York in the nineteenth century. Famous residents have included Edward L. Godkin, reformer and founder of *The Nation*; Frederick MacMonnies, the sculptor; and Guy Pène duBois, the painter. Marcel Duchamp, the painter who amazed the art world in 1913 with his *Nude Descending a Staircase*, lived at No. 28. Kahlil Gibran, the poet who wrote *The Prophet*, lived further down West 10th Street, at No. 51; Sinclair Lewis lived at No. 37.

Three-story No. 58 West 10th Street [15; opposite], built in 1836 and later remodeled by Stanford White, was the residence of Hamilton Fish Armstrong, author of *Those Days* and a distinguished scholar of foreign affairs. In the rear of the property stands a second house, originally separate from No. 58, but now joined to it. This house was once the home of the Tile Club, in its day the city's foremost artists' society. Its members included the leading artists of the late nineteenth and early twentieth centuries, among them Stanford White, the architect; Augustus Saint-Gaudens and Daniel Chester French, the sculptors; and William Merritt Chase, the painter. To the left is No. 56, a well-preserved late Federal town house owned by painter Saul Schary.

On March 5, 1970, the elegant Italianate town house at No. 18 West 11th Street, once the home of lyricist Howard Dietz, was rocked by an explosion. Within minutes it was a smoldering ruin. Several young men and women, members of the radical underground Weathermen faction, had been making bombs in the cellar, and one had gone off accidentally. The architect Hugh Hardy designed a building for himself on the site, but the Landmarks Commission, which must pass all designs for the Greenwich Village Historic District, took so long in evaluating the project that rising construction costs forced Hardy to abandon his plan. The design was, however, taken up by new clients and was finally completed in 1979. The new house [16; right] is a topic of debate: is it too modern for the row in which it stands or not modern enough?

A small triangular yard with a few gravestones on West 11th Street just east of Sixth Avenue is all that remains of the second cemetery of Congregation Shearith Israel [17]. The greenery and gently aging tombstones form a pleasant contrast to the street's elegant red-brick town houses and the bustling sidewalks and traffic of the nearby avenue. Originally a rectangular plot, the cemetery was founded in 1805 in rural Greenwich Village when the congregation's first burial ground, just south of Chatham Square, was closed for lack of space. When West 11th Street was put through in 1830, a large section of the graveyard was eliminated. The congregation then established its third cemetery uptown on Love Lane (now 21st Street). In 1852 any further interments within the city limits were prohibited. Today the three Shearith Israel cemeteries stand as a reminder of the city's relentless northward growth and of its early Jewish population.

No. 47 Fifth Avenue [18; left] is the only mid-nineteenth-century mansion on lower Fifth Avenue to survive with its facade and imposing stoop intact. Built in 1852–53 for Irad Hawley, the mansion offers a glimpse into the life-style of the city's richest families during the nineteenth century. The parlor floor, which is open to the public on weekday afternoons, boasts elaborate white marble mantels with statuary, lush plaster ceiling ornamentation, rosewood doors and two pairs of Corinthian columns between the front and back parlors. Since 1917 the building has housed the Salmagundi Club, founded in 1871 and now America's oldest artists' club.

The First Presbyterian Church [19; opposite], built in 1844–46, occupies the blockfront of Fifth Avenue between West 11th and West 12th Streets. The handsome Gothic Revival structure was designed by Joseph C. Wells, an Englishman who was later one of the founders of the American Institute of Architects; the tower is modeled on that of Magdalen College in Oxford, England. The cast-iron railings, dating from the early nineteenth century, come from the congregation's original location at Wall Street. The remodeling of the South Parish House was one of the earlier works of McKim, Mead and White (1893). The Church House, a corner of which is visible in the right foreground, was designed by Edgar Tafel and completed in 1960. Standing on the site of the studio where John Rogers created the small statuary groups so popular during the last half of the nineteenth century, it blends harmoniously with the church and the adjacent houses on West 12th Street. The church and its verdant grounds separate the stretch of distinguished high-rise apartment buildings to the south from the office buildings and shops to the north of 12th Street.

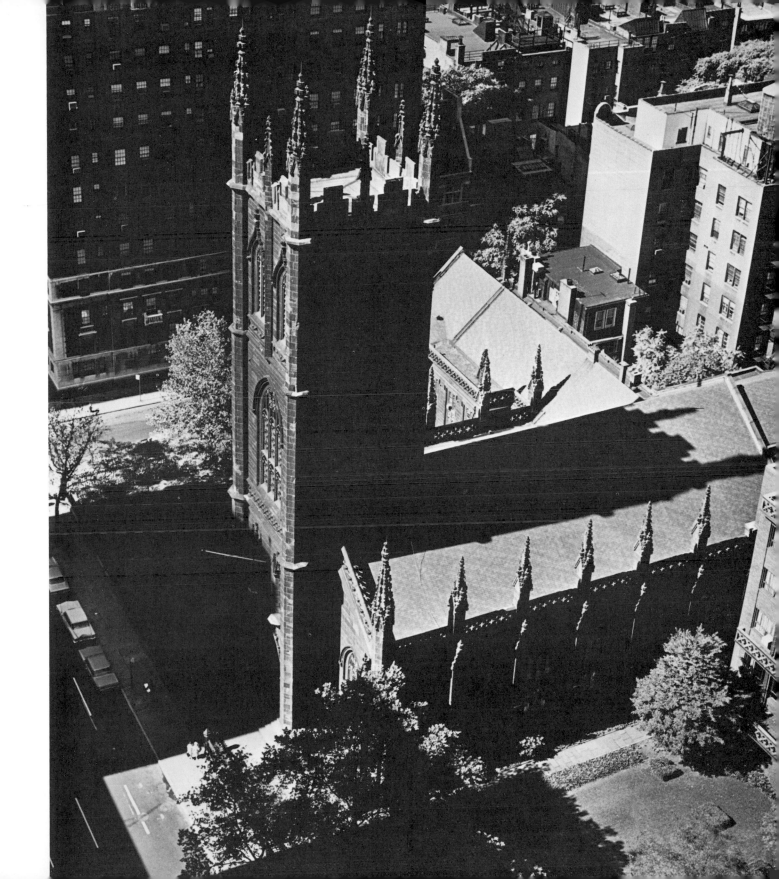

No. 24 West 12th Street [20, opposite] a handsome building in the Anglo-Italianate style, was built in 1851. Two years later it was purchased by General Winfield Scott, a hero of the Mexican War. Today it houses a branch of Odyssey House, a drug rehabilitation community. The entrance is one of the most elegant in the Village; its iron railings date from the 1880s. In 1975 the building was designated a national historic landmark.

At Asti's, No. 13 East 12th Street [21; below], an Italian meal is usually punctuated by operatic arias sung by members of the staff. Customers are encouraged to make their own musical contributions to the evening. At No. 7 is Fairchild Publications, publisher of several trade magazines, including *Women's Wear Daily*, a newspaper beloved by New Yorkers for its coverage of the fashion scene, its reviews, and choice bits of gossip.

Joseph Urban's building for the New School for Social Research at No. 66 West 12th Street [22; right], with its severe horizontal emphasis and striated brickwork, recalls the architectural avant-garde of the 1930s. Urban, a multi-talented artist who applied his gifts to designing theaters, theatrical settings, houses, cars and furniture, sought to make the structure compatible with its neighboring mid-nineteenth-century town houses by recessing the top floors and narrowing the lowest band of windows. The building contains works by the noted muralists José Clemente Orozco and Thomas Hart Benton. The school, founded in 1919 as a pioneering effort in adult education, became a gathering place for intellectuals who fled Nazi Germany. Erwin Piscator, the great director, was one refugee who joined the faculty. As the New School has prospered and grown, it has acquired real estate and spread out in a manner similar to N.Y.U.

The Dauber & Pine Bookshops, No. 66 Fifth Avenue [23; opposite], has long been a favorite browsing place for those in quest of old and rare books. It was saved from demolition in 1973 by the protests of scholars, bibliophiles and publishers. The building also houses the Parsons School of Design. Theatrical producer John Houseman lived in a penthouse at No. 66 at the time of the 1929 crash. In his memoir, *Runthrough*, he tells of some of the other residents in the building— Martha Graham and Carl Van Doren as well as some less reputable personages. The Boni Brothers ran their publishing house here, as did The Macmillan Company, which moved next door to John Russell Pope's building at No. 60 Fifth Avenue (now the home of *Forbes Magazine*) in 1925.

The interior of Dauber & Pine [right top]. Bargains like these are generally available in one corner of the basement level, while the opposite corner, with rare and abstruse tomes, is frequented by scholars in all areas of learning.

The Cinemabilia book store, No. 10 West 13th Street [24; right bottom] is one of Greenwich Village's specialty shops with an international clientele. The variety and quality of the material it carries on the movie industry—rare items, new books and magazines, stills and ephemera— make it a valued resource for film buffs and scholars.

The Village Community Church [25; opposite], an outstanding example of the Greek Revival Style, stands on the exceptionally handsome block of West 13th Street between Sixth and Seventh Avenues. Erected in 1846, the church was carefully rebuilt according to Samuel Thompson's original design after devastating fires in 1855 and 1902. Dr. Samuel D. Burchard was rector of the church—then known as the Thirteenth Street Presbyterian Church—when he made his famous "Rum, Romanism, and Rebellion" speech which backfired and helped assure James Blaine's loss of the Presidential election of 1884 to Grover Cleveland. In 1980 plans were made to convert the structure, which was no longer used as a church, into apartments. No. 152, also on the block, housed the office of *The Dial*, a leading magazine of arts and letters in the 1920s.

The first Catholic Hospital to open in the city (1849), St. Vincent's at Seventh Avenue and West 11th Street [26; above], has

a distinguished record of service. The staff of the hospital treated battlefield casualties brought to New York during the Civil War, and wrote a standard text on operating procedures for inexperienced doctors drafted into service. In 1899 the hospital used the country's first automobile ambulance. Soft-top ambulances belonging to the hospital broke the fall of panicked workers who leapt from windows during the infamous Triangle fire in 1911. The following year survivors of the *Titanic* were treated at the hospital. The hospital has touched the lives of many famous people. Georges Clemenceau, the "Old Tiger," studied medicine there in 1866. While still in office, President Grover Cleveland had most of his cancerous left jaw removed by hospital surgeons. Dylan Thomas died there in 1953. Edna St. Vincent Millay was given her middle name because the hospital had saved the life of a relative. Today it is noted for its work in the field of heart disease and plastic surgery. This building, one of several belonging to the hospital, was completed in 1899.

Gourmet foods and choice produce make Balducci's [26A; left top], No. 424 Sixth Avenue, a favorite with shoppers from all over the city. During the summer, carts are set out in front of the store to sell ices and cooling drinks to hot pedestrians.

Many streets converge at the Village Square [left bottom]. Here Christopher Street runs into Greenwich Avenue, which in turn meets Sixth Avenue. In the background, starting at Sixth Avenue, is 8th Street, which runs east past Broadway and terminates at Astor Place.

The Jefferson Market Courthouse [27; opposite] rises above the traffic at Sixth Avenue and West 10th Street. Completed in 1876, the red-brick courthouse, with its fire-lookout tower and clock, is all that remains of a complex by Vaux and Withers that also included a market and jail. It was built in the Victorian Gothic mode—an exuberant mixture of many historical architectural styles—and is generally considered one of the nation's finest pieces of architecture surviving from the period. Unused since 1945, the courthouse was threatened with demolition but, because of public outcry, was extensively remodeled in 1967 and reopened as a branch of the New York Public Library. It features exhibitions and services that benefit the Village community.

West 10th Street between Greenwich Avenue and Waverly Place offers a sampling of Village architecture: late Federal houses, a Romanesque Revival firehouse and an apartment house of 1903—Nos. 135–137 [28; opposite] showing some exceptionally fine carved stone ornamentation. At the Ninth Circle, a bar next door, Edward Albee saw the phrase "Who's afraid of Virginia Woolf?" written on a mirror. He later used it as the title of his award-winning play. The section of West 10th Street between Greenwich Avenue and the Hudson was originally named Amos Street after the farmer whose property the road ran through.

Milligan Place [above left] is an oasis of small houses, trees and quiet, just steps off the west side of Sixth Avenue between West 10th and West 11th Streets. The story is told that Aaron D. Patchin was hired to survey land for Samuel Milligan, who owned, among other properties, both Milligan Place (then Milligan Lane) and what is now Patchin Place. Patchin fell in love with Milligan's daughter, Isabella, and managed to acquire both a wife and land at the same time. In 1852 he had the modest three-story brick houses built. The Basque waiters and

workmen of the old Hotel Brevoort on lower Fifth Avenue are reputed to have lived here. According to another Village legend, Milligan Place housed French feather workers who spent their days curling ostrich and egret plumes. George Cram Cook, founder of the Provincetown Players, lived here with his wife, Pulitzer-prize-winning playwright Susan Glaspell, from 1913 until 1917.

Secluded Patchin Place [above right] just off West 10th Street, opposite towered and gabled Jefferson Market Courthouse. These ten modestly detailed red-brick houses were built in 1848 by Aaron D. Patchin. Theodore Dreiser lived here, as did John Reed, whose *Ten Days That Shook the World* (written while he was living at No. 147 West 4th Street) is a classic on the Russian Revolution. Reed is buried within the Kremlin in Moscow. Patchin Place's strongest association was with e. e. cummings, who lived and wrote his poems at No. 4 for forty years until his death in 1962. Carl Van Doren moved into No. 123 West 10th Street, just around the corner, in 1927.

Village night spots—from small and cozy to big and brassy—cater to every taste and pocket. Trude Heller's [29; left] on Sixth Avenue and 9th Street, just off the Village Square, is an old favorite.

Because of its reputation for tolerance and a progressive attitude, the Village has for many years contained a large homosexual community. The Oscar Wilde Memorial Bookshop [30; below left], No. 15 Christopher Street, stocks books and publications with a "gay" slant. The building in which it is housed was erected as part of a row in 1827. The basement shop, which now features a needlework gallery, was opened in 1924.

Christopher Street between Gay Street and Waverly Place [opposite top] offers a fine cross section of Village architecture. No. 14 (left), built in 1896–97 but recently modernized, sports attractive balconies and picture windows on its upper floors. The ground floor is notable for its tall display window. To the right of it stands No. 16, a Federal house built in 1828 (third story added later). Nos. 18 and 20, the two houses next door, built in the same year, have retained their original dormers (obscured by foliage) as well as charming wooden shopfronts that were added later in the century. Following a trend that is finding increasing favor in the Village, the handsome loft building at the end of the block, completed in 1900, has recently been converted into a luxury apartment house.

The view of West Fourth Street [opposite bottom], taken from Jones Street, belies the area's hectic pace. No. 181 (left) was originally built as a one-story stable in 1852; the renovation into its present form was made in 1872. Nos. 175–179 were built in 1833–34 on the site of a slaughterhouse. While Nos. 177 and 179 have retained their Federal dormers, No. 175 has had a full top story added. Although shops occupy the ground floor of the buildings, the facades have not been mutilated by modernization.

The sober three-sided red-brick Northern Dispensary [31; opposite], at the intersection of Christopher Street and Waverly Place, is the oldest infirmary in the city, dating from 1831. Village residents founded the institution in 1827 to provide health care for poor residents in the area—then the northern edge of the city. Edgar Allan Poe was treated for a head cold here free of charge in 1837. Other patients have included Artemus Ward, President Lincoln's favorite humorist, and Jenny Lind, the "Swedish Nightingale," whose appearance at Castle Garden in 1850 (her American debut) greatly excited the city. Only within the skewed streets of the West Village could Waverly Place intersect Waverly Place. Actually, Waverly Place splits in two when it reaches the triangular Northern Dispensary at Christopher Street. Elsewhere, the confused jumble of Village Streets features an intersection of West 4th and West 11th Streets. Most of the village escaped the grid plan imposed on New York in 1811 because plots had already developed according to old property lines.

Christopher Park [above], a tiny island of trees and benches, lies just north of Sheridan Square. Frequent attempts to clear derelicts out of the park have met with little success. Named after Civil War General Philip Sheridan, whose statue, done in 1936 by Joseph P. Pollia, stands in the background, the park offers the Villager an amalgam of modern high-rise buildings, nineteenth-century houses, shops and restaurants. The El Avram, at the far right, specializes in Israeli cabaret. The square was the scene of some of the bloodiest fighting during the draft riots of July 16–19, 1863. It is said that a house-owner on Grove Street hid blacks in his basement to prevent the mob from killing them. (By the time the riots were over, eighteen Blacks had been lynched in the city.)

McNulty's [32; left] sells the "world's choicest coffees" and "rare Oriental teas" at No. 109 Christopher Street. The appearance of the store, with its fixtures, plate-glass display windows, pressed-metal column and cellar opening into the sidewalk, has changed little since the business was established in 1895.

Standing at the corner of Christopher and Greenwich Streets, the massive ten-story U.S. Federal Building [33A; below right] is one of New York's few examples of the Chicago School of architecture. Designed by Willoughby J. Edbrooke and erected in 1899, the Romanesque Revival building originally served as the Customs Appraisers' Warehouse. Having served for years as the local post office and as a storage house for records from the National Archives, it stands empty as Villagers heatedly argue about plans for its future use. In early years, Greenwich Street was the main road linking the city downtown with the then-rural Village.

The handsome Federal facade of St. John's Lutheran Church [33; below left], No. 81 Christopher Street,

stands in quiet contrast to the boutiques and restaurants that proliferate along the street. Built in 1821–22 as the Eighth Presbyterian Church, the building underwent some alteration in 1886, but preserves its essential characteristics, most notably its distinctive octagonal tower.

The sign at the Li-Lac Candy store [34; right] at No. 120 Christopher Street says "New French Chocolate Co.," but the shop has been purveying its delectable products to faithful gourmets from the Village and the entire city since 1923.

The Theatre De Lys [35; below], on Christopher Street, has been the home of many fine off-Broadway presentations. During the 1950s, it housed the enormously successful revival of *The Threepenny Opera*, which had all New York whistling "The Ballad of Mack the Knife."

The White Horse Tavern [36; opposite] has occupied the early nineteenth-century building at Hudson and West 11th Streets since 1880. Long a favorite with young writers, it was one of Dylan Thomas' haunts.

The Abingdon Square playground [above], renovated in 1966, offers a retreat for some of the Village's children, chess players, and derelicts. Little visible remains of the square's history.

Originally part of the property of Sir Peter Warren, who came to New York City in 1730 and who owned substantial tracts of the Village, the square is named after Willoughby, Earl of Abingdon, who married Charlotte, Warren's eldest daughter. Little remains of the charming houses of the 1830s that once surrounded the square. Today's view is dominated by high-rise apartment buildings and nondescript holdovers from the late nineteenth century.

Les Trois Provinces [37; left], one of the many antique shops on Bleecker Street near Abingdon Square, tempts collectors with its fine French country furniture.

Built in 1836, the ten houses at Nos. 301–319 West 4th Street [below], between Bank and West 12th Streets, comprise one of the oldest extant blocks in the Village. All the houses were built in the Greek Revival style, but only three, Nos. 303, 309, and 313, have maintained their original one-and-a-half-story height. The variety of fine wrought-iron railings adds to the houses' charm. Farther up the street, at No. 238, Edward Albee wrote *The Zoo Story*. Bank Street received its name in the early nineteenth century, when the banks of New York City, along with other businesses, moved north to Greenwich Village during the yellow-fever epidemics that ravaged the city.

Ye Waverly Inn [38; opposite], established in 1920, is probably the most "typically American" restaurant in New York City, according to *The New York Times*. Tucked into the ground floor of a town house at No. 16 Bank Street, the restaurant has low ceilings, country furniture, and wide plank floors. The food features such home-style dishes as roast beef, meat loaf, and chicken pot pie. Willa Cather wrote *My Antonia* while living at No. 5 Bank Street (demolished).

Operating at the northern edge of the Village and maintaining its nineteenth-century atmosphere is the Gansevoort Meat Market [left], one of the last great markets remaining in the city. On a dock close by, Herman Melville worked for 19 years as a customs inspector after his attempts at a literary career had failed.

The Old Homestead Steak House [39; below], at No. 56 Ninth Avenue near 14th Street, stands at the northern edge of the Village. Founded in 1868, the restaurant is New York's oldest steak house.

This group of handsome town houses on Jane Street [right] between Eighth Avenue and Hudson Street dates from the late 1840s and exemplifies the charm of the West Village. No. 52 (with the white doorway) was the home of Edna St. Vincent Millay for a time.

Westbeth [40; below], No. 463 West Street, at Bethune, is a prime example of how an old building can be redeveloped for new uses. Originally the structure housed the Bell Telephone Laboratories. Here Bell scientists made fundamental advances in magnetism, acoustics and electronics and created the systems required for universal telephony. While housed in the building they also learned how to send thousands of communications over the same physical path simultaneously; they originated sound movies, hi-fi, and long-distance television transmission; they invented the first electrical digital and analog computers. When Bell moved to New Jersey, the building was converted into spacious apartments for artists. West Street is also the site of a new development of low-rise housing.

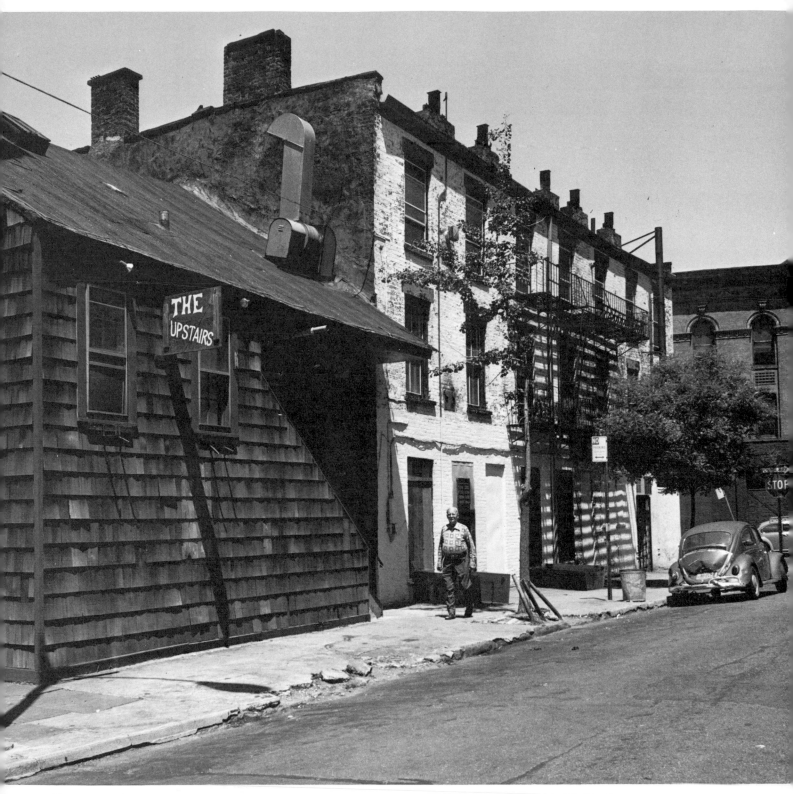

Although greatly altered, parts of the little frame house at No. 6 Weehawken Street [41; opposite], near the Hudson River, survive from the eighteenth century and serve as a reminder of the Village's long-vanished rustic past. The earliest settlement in the area, located at what is now the foot of Gansevoort Street, had already been established by Indians when Henry Hudson first explored the region in 1609.

No. 121 Charles Street [42; above], which may date from the eighteenth century, was moved from an unknown location to York Avenue and 71st Street sometime during the nineteenth century. When it was threatened with demolition in the early 1960s to make way for a high-rise building, its owner purchased this corner lot and had the house moved there, where, hopefully, its travels have come to an end. It is a strange sight to see the modest country house sitting on its plot, completely indifferent to its commercial surroundings.

Even though the West Side Highway runs overhead nearby, and the view consists mainly of rotting piers and grimy industry on the New Jersey side of the Hudson, in good weather the waterfront in the area around the foot of Christopher and Morton Streets [opposite top] attracts Villagers seeking sun, air and relative quiet. This locale has been appreciated as a retreat ever since the early years of the nineteenth century, when the New York State Prison was located nearby at the foot of West 10th Street. In 1801, it was reported that "a more pleasant airy and salubrious spot could not have been selected in the vicinity of New York." The waterfront's bars and rundown hotels linger on as vestiges of the once prosperous maritime trade.

The view down Grove Street [opposite bottom], where it makes a gentle curve between Bedford and Hudson Streets, and ends at St. Luke's Chapel, is one of the most picturesque in the city. The row houses at Nos. 2½–10 Grove Street, dating from the 1820s and 1830s and seen here on the left, still retain the modest doors with rectangular toplights, hand-wrought ironwork and dormer windows characteristic of the city's domestic Federal style. The row at Nos. 12–18 offers some fine examples of the Greek Revival style of the 1840s.

St. Luke's Episcopal Chapel [43; below] on Hudson Street at the foot of Grove Street is the city's third oldest church. The oldest is St. Paul's, followed by St. Mark's in the Bowery. Clement C. Moore, author of "The Night Before Christmas," was the first warden of St. Luke's. When the severe Federal-style church, attributed variously to John Heath or James N. Wells, was built in 1821–1822, it was surrounded by open fields and occasional frame houses and was known as St. Luke's-in-the-Fields. Although it faces busy Hudson Street, the chapel sits in a quiet garden-like park which it shares with a few brick row houses of the 1820s that are now occupied by the fashionable St. Luke's School, founded in 1894. One of the row houses bears a plaque indicating that it was the boyhood home of Bret Harte, short-story writer, novelist and poet. In the background looms the U.S. Federal Building. Villagers may object to its size, but standing in contrast to St. Luke's, it demonstrates the variety and vitality of New York architecture.

Grove Court [44; left and below], one of the hidden delights of Greenwich Village, is entered through a gate and passageway between Nos. 10 and 12 Grove Street. The Grove Court houses were built in the 1850s for workingmen. Significantly, the court became known as "Mixed Ale Alley." The Court provided O. Henry with the inspiration to write his story "The Last Leaf."

No. 17 Grove Street [45; opposite] (corner of Bedford) is one of the few remaining frame houses in Greenwich Village. It was built in 1822 for William Hyde, a window-sash maker. His little workshop, frequently and incorrectly identified as old slave quarters, was built in 1833 and still stands around the corner at the back of the house. Over the years, the house has undergone several modernizations—a Greek Revival style doorway in the 1830s or 1840s, a third story and protruding cornice in 1870, and later a disfiguring but necessary fire-escape.

Though sadly altered today, No. 45 Grove Street [46; opposite], built in 1830, was one of the finest mansions in Greenwich Village. Its arched fanlight doorway and, at the end of the stoop railings, the iron torchères which lighted the entrance at night, recall the glories of the Federal style. This forty-seven-foot-wide dwelling originally was the home of Samuel Whittemore, who owned much land in the Village. In the early nineteenth century, the house stood on spacious grounds with a water cistern, well, hothouse, and stables. After several changes in ownership, the surrounding grounds were sold in the 1850s for development. The mansion itself was converted into shops and apartments in the 1870s. The poet Hart Crane lived in the building in 1923. At No. 49, Vance Bourjaily hosted a group that included William Styron, Gore Vidal and Louis Auchincloss.

The attractive little house at No. 70 Bedford Street [47; above left] has undergone many alterations since it was built in 1807 for John P. Roome, a sailmaker and "crier of the courts of oyer and terminer and gaol delivery and of the general session of the peace." A third story was added where there had originally been an attic with dormers, and a lintel marks the position of the original Federal-style doorway.

In 1926, the building at No. 86 Bedford Street [48; above right] was purchased by Lee Chumley, an enterprising gentleman. He altered the front of the building to make it look like a garage, but behind its doors he ran a speakeasy that attracted Village notables such as Edna St. Vincent Millay, John Dos Passos and Theodore Dreiser. Today a restaurant operates behind a facade altered yet again. To commemorate the prohibition era, it is named Chumley's, and does not post its name outside the door.

No. 77 Bedford Street [49; left], at the corner of Commerce Street, is thought to be the oldest surviving house in Greenwich Village. Built in 1799–1801, its first two occupants—Joshua Isaacs and Harmon Hendricks—were pioneers in copper-rolling who also acted as New York agents for Paul Revere. The house has undergone substantial alteration over the past years, including the addition of a brick facade and a third-story studio. The house next to it, at No. 75½ Bedford Street [50], has the distinction of being the narrowest house in the Village: it is only 9½ feet wide. Built in 1873 on the site of an alley located between the two buildings and leading to a rear court and stable yard, it was the home of Edna St. Vincent Millay in 1923–24. Much of the property on Bedford Street was at one time owned by Aaron Burr, who speculated heavily in Village property, without much success.

The "Twin Peaks" at No. 102 Bedford Street [51; opposite] is "pure Hansel and Gretel," according to the *AIA Guide to New York City*. Built c. 1830, the building originally was a frame house with the pitched roof and dormer windows of the Federal style. In 1925, Village resident Clifford Reed Daily—with the backing of Otto Kahn, the banker and art patron—remodeled the building into a pseudo-medieval architectural extravaganza. Renovator Daily reputedly believed the surrounding area was "unfit for inspiring the minds of creative Villagers" and decided to build this "island growing in a desert of mediocrity."

Commerce Street, between Bedford and Barrow Streets, has an abrupt right-angle turn in mid-block and features the diversified buildings so characteristic of much of the Village. The Cherry Lane Theatre at No. 38 [52; opposite top] was founded as an experimental theater by Edna St. Vincent Millay and her friends in a building originally erected as a brewery in 1836. Mark Van Doren shared his first Village apartment with Joseph Wood Krutch at nearby No. 43 Barrow Street.

The twin houses at Nos. 39 and 41 Commerce Street [53; opposite bottom] and their common garden add a touch of Paris to the Village. According to a cherished legend, they were built by a sea captain for his two daughters who could not get along well enough to share a home. The truth is more prosaic—they were built in 1831–1832 for a milkman. The mansard roofs were later additions. The Cherry Lane Theatre stands in the background; to the right is the Blue Mill Tavern [54], favored by Villagers for its simple but hearty fare.

No. 7 Leroy Street [55; right], a fine Federal house of 1830, now stands between a store window and a garage door. An architectural feature that can be seen on many of the Village's houses of the period is the old "horsewalk" marked by the small door at the sidewalk level to the left of the stoop. The door opens on an enclosed alley which led to a stable in the back yard where nineteenth-century New Yorkers kept their horses.

St. Luke's Place [above left] is one of the most delightful streets in all of New York. The nicely landscaped red-brick-front houses in the Italianate style of the 1850s are set back from the street. Residents of St. Luke's Place have included the sculptor Theodore Roszab (No. 1), the painter Paul Cadmus (No. 5), Theodore Dreiser (No. 16) and Sherwood Anderson (No. 12). Poet Marianne Moore lived at No. 14 and worked around the corner at the Hudson Park branch of the New York Public Library. The street was used for exterior shots in the movie *Wait Until Dark*.

James J. Walker, flamboyant mayor of New York City from 1926 to 1933, made his home at No. 6 St. Luke's Place [56; above right]. The two "lamps of honor"—a traditional way to mark the home of a mayor—remain on the newel posts. The custom may go back to Dutch times.

In 1902 Mary K. Simkhovitch established Greenwich House to provide the area around Jones Street—then the most densely populated block on the lower West Side—with social services, especially for children. In 1917 the institution opened this handsome Neo-Federal building at No. 27 Barrow Street [57; opposite]. Greenwich House continues to serve the Village. It features a child-care program, a counseling center for drug addicts, an evening program of adult education, a music school, a pottery school, and a center for senior citizens. It also sponsors free art shows, concerts, and a summer camp for children and the elderly.

Our Lady of Pompeii Church [58; opposite] was built on Carmine Street in 1926 on the site of a church where St. Frances Xavier Cabrini, patron saint of immigrants and the first American citizen to be canonized, was a worshipper. The children who attend the church's parochial school frequently crowd the streets, jamming the neighborhood's pizza parlors at lunchtime. In the autumn the church sponsors a fair along Carmine Street, and a ferris wheel is set up in Father Demo Square on Sixth Avenue (foreground).

The jars that line the walls of Aphrodisia Products [59; right top], No. 28 Carmine Street, are filled with a profusion of herbs and spices. One of the Village's many specialty stores, the shop carries on an extensive mail-order trade.

On Carmine Street [right bottom], which runs between Father Demo Square and Seventh Avenue South, neighborhood service stores exist side by side with more exotic shops having a city-wide clientele. The street maintains an Italian accent with several restaurants and a bakery. Edgar Allan Poe lived briefly at No. 113½ (demolished).

The small red-brick houses on the north side of Charlton Street [opposite], just south of Houston Street, form the longest stretch of Federal-style dwellings of the 1820s and 1830s remaining in New York City. King and Vandam Streets boast similar houses—all lovingly maintained or restored by their present occupants. The area marks the site of one of early New York's most famous estates, Richmond Hill, shown [below] in a lithograph from *Valentine's Manual*, 1856. The mansion had been built in 1767 by Major Abraham Mortier. It served as headquarters for Washington in 1776 and was the home of John Adams in 1789 while he was Vice President. Abigail Adams wrote of it:

> *In natural beauty it might vie with the most delicious spot I ever saw. . . . The house stands upon an eminence; at an agreeable distance flows the noble Hudson. . . . Venerable oaks and broken ground covered with wild shrubs surround me, giving a natural beauty to the spot which is truly enchanting. A lovely variety of birds serenade me morning and evening, rejoicing in their liberty and security.*

Richmond Hill was later purchased by Aaron Burr, and it was from the mansion that he set forth on the morning of July 11, 1804, for the Weehawken Heights in New Jersey, where he fatally wounded Alexander Hamilton in a duel. Thereafter, the house went into a decline. The 100-foot hill upon which it stood was cut out from under it, and in 1822 the pillared mansion, where dignitaries ranging from Indian chiefs to Talleyrand had been entertained, was turned into a tavern. It was briefly used as a theater and finally, in 1849, was razed.

In the 1920s, while she enjoyed a period of great productivity, the poet Edna St. Vincent Millay lived in this fine Federal house at No. 25 Charlton Street [60; right].

The house at the corner of Prince and Macdougal Streets has undergone many alterations. Its neighbor at No. 203 Prince Street [61; above] has benefited from a sympathetic restoration revealing many of the features that mark it as transitional from Federal to Greek Revival. It was built in 1833–34 for John H. Haff, a leather inspector, on land that had belonged to Aaron Burr. The third story, replacing its original dormers, was added later in the century. The area once boasted many such houses, but in the 1850s the middle class abandoned the neighborhood as its character became increasingly commercial. The house stands on the edge of SoHo, which is bounded by Houston Street on the north, Canal Street on the south, West Broadway on the west and Broadway on the east. Declared an historic district because of its great wealth of cast-iron buildings, in recent years it has become a home for artists and the galleries that show their work.

Crowds pack Sullivan Street annually during the week of June 13th, lured by the Italian atmosphere of the Feast of St. Anthony of Padua. The church [62; opposite], on the corner of West Houston and Sullivan Streets, is the saint's national shrine. Amusements, games of chance and food stalls line the sidewalks between West Houston and Spring Streets, adding great color and excitement to the neighborhood.

A staggering amount of food is sold at the feast. Pizza, lasagna, clams, sausages and peppers, lobster, calzoni, corn, watermelon and beer quickly sate even the most voracious appetite. Here zeppole, pastries similar to doughnuts, simmer in deep fat before they are taken out, dusted with confectioner's sugar, and sold in paper bags which absorb excess grease. Another booth offers torrone—a rich nougat—and strings of nuts.

Although many visitors to the street fair may tend to forget it, the Feast of St. Anthony of Padua is primarily a religious event. At the procession marking the beginning of the feast, the saint's image is carried through the streets and the faithful make contributions by pinning money to the ribbons attached to it.

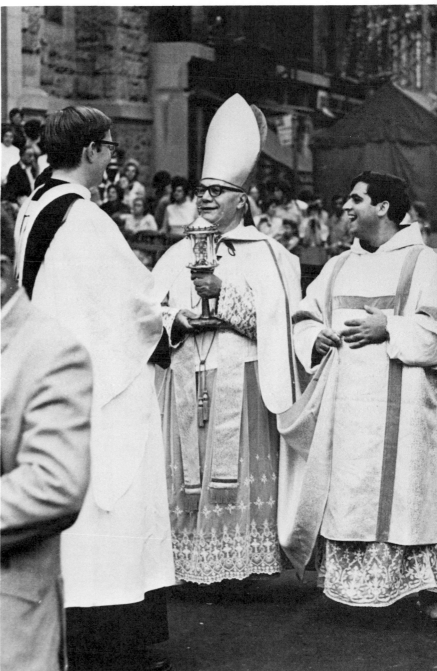

74

The Fantasticks, which has played at the Sullivan Street Playhouse [63; opposite left] since its opening on May 3, 1960, proudly bills itself as the world's longest-running musical. The house at No. 177 was the birthplace of Fiorello LaGuardia, New York's colorful and progressive mayor from 1934 to 45.

Bleecker Street, which runs from Abingdon Square to the Bowery, contains homes, shops, schools, restaurants, theaters and night spots. Many of the stores, such as this one near Jones Street [opposite right], display their choice and bargain merchandise "al fresco." At the curb is one of New York's dwindling number of pushcarts.

Many of the shops along Bleecker Street just east and west of Sixth Avenue attest to the thriving Italian community in the area south of Washington Square. Like the larger "Little Italy" on the Lower East Side, this neighborhood has maintained a distinct ethnic flavor over the years. Italian-Americans who now live in other parts of the city continue to come here to shop, eat, pray and socialize. Delicious breads of varying sizes and shapes fill the window of A. Zito & Sons at No. 259 Bleecker Street [64; right]. Along with other Italian bakeries in the Village, such as Zampieri Bros. at No. 17 Cornelia Street and Bruno's Bakery Corp., No. 506 La Guardia Place, it supplies restaurants throughout the city with the toast rounds and bread sticks that their diners munch with cocktails.

The heady aroma of choice blends of coffee lures the passerby into the Porto Rico Importing Company, No. 201 Bleecker Street [65; above left]. Since its opening in 1907, the store has been a mecca for coffee and tea fanciers throughout the city.

The Circle in the Square [66; above right] has become a fixed feature of New York's theatrical life. The company takes its name from its original home in Sheridan Square where it presented plays in the round. It has since grown to encompass two theaters, this one at No. 159 Bleecker Street and one midtown, on 50th Street. The Circle in the Square has presented works by playwrights such as Jean Genet, Thornton Wilder and Christopher Fry.

The Little Red School House at No. 196 Bleecker Street [67; above left], just east of Sixth Avenue, was founded in 1932 by Elisabeth Irwin, a pioneer in progressive education. For over thirty years, the private school has made significant contributions to educational concepts.

No. 160 Bleecker Street [68; above right], between Thompson and Sullivan Streets, has had a long and checkered career since it was built in 1896. It was designed by one of New York's most influential architects, Ernest Flagg, as Mills House No. 1, a hotel endowed by philanthropist Darius Ogden Mills as a place where poor transients could find clean, adequate lodging for twenty cents a night. Each of the 1500 rooms (one bed to each) had a window looking either outside or onto one of the two large interior courts. Theodore Dreiser stayed there when he first came to New York. In later years, as the Greenwich Hotel, the building harbored a derelict clientele that so terrorized the neighborhood that the building was eventually shut down. Today it has been renovated and reopened as The Atrium, a luxury apartment house. The Village Gate and The Top of the Gate are two popular cabarets, both under the same management, which operate in the building. James Fenimore Cooper, author of *The Last of the Mohicans*, lived across the street at No. 145 after his return from Europe in 1833.

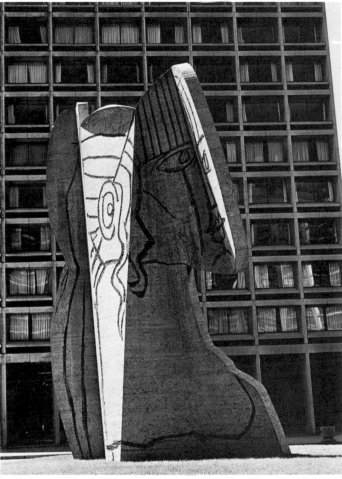

The Village is rich in movie houses featuring revivals of American and foreign film classics. The Bleecker Street Cinema [69; above left], at No. 144, has offered such programs for many years. The building's elegant facade dates from 1920–24, when architect Raymond Hood (later to design the Daily News Building) created it for Mori's Restaurant, which had been a Village fixture since 1884.

The 36-foot-high *Bust of Sylvette* [70; above right], is New

York's only monumental sculpture designed by Picasso (adaptation and execution were carried out by Carl Nesjar). The work stands in the middle of I. M. Pei's acclaimed University Village, a group of three apartment towers built in 1966. Many members of the N.Y.U. faculty live there.

At night the neon-lighted blocks of Bleecker Street south of Washington Square come alive with pedestrians going to restaurants, shops, theaters and cabarets. At nearby No. 172 writer James Agee had an apartment between 1941 and 1951.

THE DUGOUT

TAVERN

RESTAURANT →DOWNSTAIRS

BITTER END

THE BITTER E.. DUGOUT

RECORDS

INDIAN

Golden Pakistan RESTA

The Minetta Brook was one of Manhattan's many waterways that have vanished from view. Originating uptown, the brook flowed through the site of Washington Square, along Minetta and Downing Streets, to empty into a swamp near the Hudson between Charlton and West Houston Streets. Once noted for its trout, the brook is now completely built over. This bend in Minetta Street [opposite] follows the twist taken by the stream. The street was used for location filming of the movie *Serpico*.

Joe Gould once held forth at the Minetta Tavern, at the corner of Minetta Lane and Macdougal Street [72; right top]. A 1911 graduate of Harvard, Gould spent his life gathering stories from the characters he met in many of the city's seedier areas. These he incorporated in his "Oral History of the World," an enormous manuscript that no one was able to find after his death in 1958. The Tavern now houses a collection of Gould memorabilia.

During the late nineteenth and early twentieth centuries, the social life of many of New York's immigrant communities was dominated by organizations such as shooting clubs and choral societies. Most of them have not survived, but the Tiro a Segno [73; right bottom], a shooting club at No. 77 Macdougal Street with many distinguished Italian-American members, continues the tradition.

Traces of Federal-style doorways and lintels survive at the three buildings at Nos. 127–131 Macdougal Street [opposite], built for Aaron Burr in 1829. The Provincetown Players, a group of actors, playwrights and designers that included, at various times, Eugene O'Neill, Edna St. Vincent Millay, George Cram Cook, Susan Glaspell, Robert Edmond Jones, Miriam Hopkins and Bette Davis, performed in a converted stable on the site of No. 133 Macdougal Street. The players had originated as a summer theater in Provincetown on Cape Cod in 1915. The next year they opened a theater at No. 139 Macdougal, and moved into No. 133 two years later. Some of the works that received their premières there were *Aria da Capo* by Edna St. Vincent Millay, *Him* by e. e. cummings, and *The Emperor Jones* and *The Hairy Ape* by Eugene O'Neill. Next to the theater stood the Liberal Club, a meeting place for radicals, which sponsored a variety of activities including lectures by Margaret Sanger on birth control, readings by Sherwood Anderson of his plays, art exhibitions and a series of dances that gained considerable notoriety. In *Greenwich Village* (1917) Anna Chapin quotes Harry Kemp on the dances:

"Uptowners, outsiders, come in here . . . and think that any-thing will go in the Liberal Club! They come in here and insult

the women members, and we all end up in u free fight every week or so."

The Granados Restaurant [74], No. 125, is noted for its Galician specialties.

By night, Macdougal Street is one of Greenwich Village's busi-est and most diversified streets [above left]. In warm weather, young people from all over the city and nation parade up and down the sidewalks and enjoy the restaurants, shops, quick-food joints, and cabarets in the area. The street takes its name from a general of the Revolutionary War, as do Sullivan, Thomp-son, Wooster, Greene, and Mercer Streets. The floodlit Empire State Building can be seen in the background.

During his restless career, Edgar Allan Poe stayed at various spots in New York, several of them in the Village. In 1844 he and his wife enjoyed a brief period of comparative prosperity while living at No. 85 West 3rd Street (then No. 15 Amity Street) [75; above right]. Greatly altered today, the building has recently housed a succession of restaurants and cabarets. For its name, this recent tenant borrowed the title of one of Poe's most famous short stories.

Sixth Avenue at West 4th Street, looking north toward the Empire State Building [left]. The decor of O. Henry's Steak House [76]—butcherblock tables, floors covered with sawdust and waiters in white aprons and straw hats—is derived from the butcher's shop that once occupied the building. The restaurant takes its name from the popular short-story writer who was a habitué of the Village. The sidewalk café, one of many in the Village, is favored by patrons who like to sip a drink as they watch the passing scene. The medallions on the lampposts along Sixth Avenue bear the seals of various American countries. In 1945 the avenue was renamed the Avenue of the Americas as a goodwill gesture, but the change was never adopted by New Yorkers, virtually all of whom stubbornly continue to call the street Sixth Avenue.

The prices may be high, and men are required to wear jacket and tie, but The Coach House, No. 110 Waverly Place [77; below] is regarded as one of New York's best restaurants. The

building it is in dates from 1826. No. 112, to the right, was built at the same time, but its facade underwent heavy alteration in 1920. Everett Shinn, a leading member of the "Ashcan School" of painters, had his studio there.

The 1970s took a heavy toll in old Village restaurants. Favorite establishments such as Mother Bertolotti's, Charles and Renato's fell victim to inflation. But others hold on. Among them is Marta's [78; right], No. 75 Washington Place. Located in a fine late Greek Revival house of 1847, the restaurant has long been patronized by Villagers.

The Bottom Line [79; below], No. 14 West 4th Street, is one of the city's most popular cabarets offering jazz, rock and folk music. It is well known as a spot featuring both new talent (recording companies sometimes hire the hall for an evening to introduce a rising performer to the New York press) and established names, such as Melba Moore and Jerry Garcia.

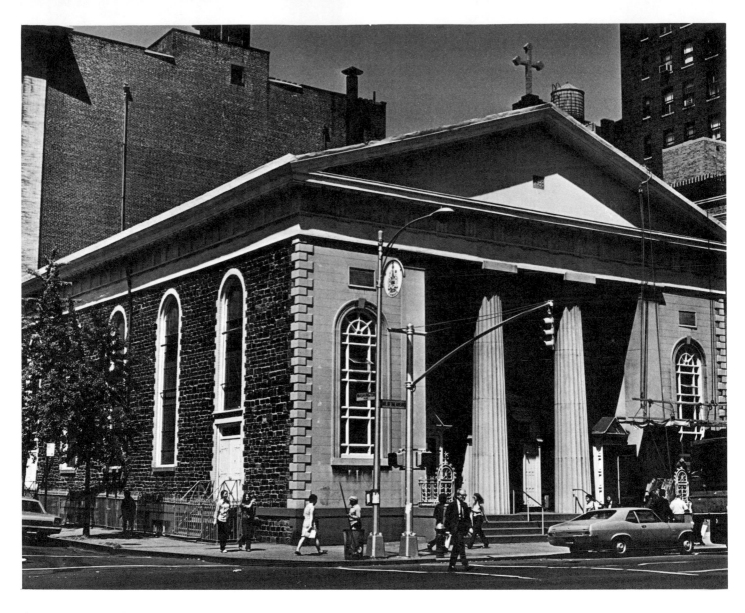

St. Joseph's Church [80; above], designed by John Doran in the Greek Revival style and built at Sixth Avenue and West Washington Place in 1833, is one of the city's oldest Roman Catholic churches. John McCloskey, who later became the first American cardinal, was an early rector here.

The Cookery [81; opposite top], on 8th Street, is a restaurant that features a sidewalk cafe. Run by Barney Josephson, who owned the famous Cafe Society in the 1930s and 1940s, the Cookery has gained an enthusiastic following of jazz buffs because of its evening performances featuring artists such as Nellie Lutcher and Rose Murphy. Brentano's, across University Place, is one of the Village's principal bookstores.

The Village Voice [82; opposite bottom], 80 University Place at East 11th Street, is a local weekly newspaper with a circulation of 145,000 and a worldwide following. A forum for liberal thought founded in 1955, it features articles on politics, civil rights and Village life, as well as drama, music and theater reviews, cartoons by Jules Feiffer, and a large classified section where the reader can find anything from a roommate to a floor-scraper. The Cedar Tavern, at No. 82, is named after the original, a favorite meeting place for such abstract-expressionist painters as Jackson Pollock and Franz Kline, which stood on University Place between East 8th and 9th Streets.

Grace Episcopal Church [83; left], at Broadway and East 10th Street, was opened in 1846. The church, designed by James Renwick, Jr., who later was the architect of St. Patrick's Cathedral on Fifth Avenue and 50th Street, is considered one of the finest Gothic-Revival structures in the United States. As one of New York's most fashionable congregations in the nineteenth century, it was the scene of many brilliant society weddings, but received greatest attention in the press for the wedding of two of P. T. Barnum's midgets, Charles Sherwood Stratton (more famous as General Tom Thumb) and Lavinia Warren Bumpus, on February 10, 1863. The building behind the church, No. 806 Broadway, was built in 1888 by Renwick's architectural firm to harmonize with the church's Gothic style. Because Broadway angles sharply to the west at 10th Street, the church forms the focal point of a long vista and can be seen from as far as a mile downtown. Legend has it that Broadway bends here because Hendrick Brevoort refused to let workmen cut the road through his farmhouse and favorite tree, defending his property with a blunderbuss. The tower in the background, capped with a large lantern, is part of the Consolidated Edison Building on 14th Street.

The handsome cast-iron building [84; opposite] that once housed the James McCreery & Co. department store dates from 1868 and stands, nearly opposite Grace Church, at Broadway and East 11th Street. Although the store stocked all kinds of fabrics for making clothes, it was most famous for its fine and expensive line of silks. After it had gone through various hands, and survived a fire, the building was converted into luxury apartments in the early 1970s, retaining many of its most charming features, including interior Corinthian columns.

At the Strand Book Store [85; above], Broadway and East 12th Street, the browsing bibliophile can enjoy one of the city's largest and most varied collections of second-hand books. Bins of books are set out on the sidewalk, but the pickings are choicer inside the jammed and often hectic store. Second-hand books can also be purchased at the nearby bookstores on Fourth Avenue, where a few stalwart dealers still uphold that thoroughfare's old reputation as New York's used-book center—something like the quais of the Seine near Notre-Dame.

Lüchow's [86; opposite], established in 1882 at No. 110 East 14th Street, stands at the northern boundary of the Village. The restaurant's facade recalls the baroque splendors of old Bavaria. Its patrons feast on German cuisine in a setting of Victorian mahogany paneling, paintings, stuffed moose and stag heads, mirrors, and murals depicting scenes from Wagner's *Ring des*

Nibelungen. Every evening diners are serenaded by an "oompah band" and a more subdued and elegant string trio. Lüchow's holds several festivals a year, complete with special decorations; at Christmas an enormous, splendidly decorated tree surrounded by a crèche, is a major attraction. Lüchow's remains virtually as it was in the 1890s, when 14th Street at Union Square was the site of Tammany Hall, and a musical and theatrical district. Seven major theaters were clustered in the immediate vicinity, among them the Academy of Music, Tony Pastor's, Steinway Hall and Amberg's (a fragment of which is still visible on Irving Place). Lüchow's has counted luminaries such as "Diamond Jim" Brady, Lillian Russell and Enrico Caruso among its regular patrons. It was at one of the restaurant's tables in 1914 that Victor Herbert, together with some friends, formed the organization that was later to become the American Society of Composers, Authors, and Publishers.

Since its completion in 1859, Cooper Union [87; opposite] in Astor Place has been one of New York's major educational assets. The Italianate brownstone building (now called Foundation Hall to distinguish it from the school's two newer buildings) was erected with funds provided by Peter Cooper, a versatile industrialist who built the first American steam locomotive and developed the iron industry. The steel that forms the Union's framework (it is the oldest extant building in America so constructed) was rolled at Cooper's mill in Trenton, which also produced the iron used in building the old Astor Library on Lafayette Street. It was in Cooper Union's Great Hall, then the largest auditorium in the city, that Abraham Lincoln made a speech on February 27, 1860, establishing himself as the leading Republican candidate for the Presidency. The institution has always had a policy of free education, giving courses in the humanities, architecture and the fine arts. Although anyone may apply, applicants must pass rigorous entrance examinations to gain admission. Adult education programs, however, as well as the many lectures sponsored by the Union, have unrestricted attendance. Distinguished alumni include Raphael Soyer, Milton Glaser, Augustus Saint-Gaudens, John Hejduk and Jack Yogman. The Union also houses the Museum for the Arts of Decoration, now a part of the Smithsonian Institution. Near the school stands a fine statue of Peter Cooper [88; above left], erected in 1897 by New York in grateful recognition of his philanthropic services. The statue

is the work of Augustus Saint-Gaudens, one of America's greatest sculptors; the canopied pedestal was the work of architect Stanford White. The Astor Place Opera House stood across the street from the Union. In 1849, the appearance there of English actor William Macready sparked the infamous Astor Place Riot in which 34 persons were killed and scores wounded.

Construction of the Astor Library on Lafayette Street [89; above right], New York's first free library, was begun in 1849 with funds left for that purpose in the will of John Jacob Astor. William Thackeray, the author of *Vanity Fair*, browsed in the library during his trips to the United States, and Washington Irving relied on its resources for his biography of Washington. In 1912 the collection was united with the Lenox Library and the Tilden Foundation to form the New York Public Library at 42nd Street and Fifth Avenue. In later years the Astor building was used as the headquarters of the Hebrew Immigrant Aid Society. Extensively renovated in 1967, the handsome Italianate building now houses several theaters where Joseph Papp stages productions. As with the Jefferson Market Courthouse and the old McCreery's, the Library demonstrates how an old building can be adapted to new uses, serving a useful function while preserving the city's architectural heritage.

Only a bedraggled remnant of the once-spectacular Colonnade Row [90; above] stands on Lafayette Street, opposite the Astor Library. Originally known as LaGrange Terrace after the country seat of the Marquis de Lafayette, the row was built in 1832–33 in an attempt to emulate the majestic terraces of London and Bath. The cutting and fitting of the Westchester marble was done by convicts from Sing Sing, causing the irate masons of New York to riot. Sold for $30,000 to $40,000 —prices then unheard-of—the buildings were occupied by families in society, such as the Delanos (Franklin D. Roosevelt's mother's family), Astors, and Vanderbilts, as well as by notables, such as Washington Irving, Peter Cooper and William Cullen Bryant. In the 1880s the fashionable world deserted the elegant Classic-Revival structure for the imitation French châteaux being built on upper Fifth Avenue. By 1902 the great trees that lined the street had been cut down, and Lafayette Place (as it had been known) had been opened up into Lafayette Street, making it a busy commercial thoroughfare. Five of the buildings at the south end of the terrace have been destroyed, and the four that remain have suffered unsightly additions and alterations. By some miracle, the lovely iron anthemion cresting that once ran along the entire roof survives at the northern end.

The Old Merchant's House [91; left], not far from Lafayette Street at No. 29 East 4th Street, is a fine example of the Greek-Revival house designed in the style of Minard Lefever. It was owned by the family of Seabury Tredwell, a prosperous merchant, from 1835—two years after the construction—until 1933, when the last descendant of the family died. It is rare for an upper-middle-class home to have been owned and lived in by one family for so long. The interior offers an opportunity to see a prosperous home of the period with furnishings intact. (The house even has two secret rooms for storing valuables.) Several years ago the house was discovered to have serious structural problems, and rain from a leaking roof and outside walls was threatening the magnificent plaster ceilings. A group of New Yorkers led by N.Y.U. architect Joseph Roberto have raised over $100,000 to save the house. Work went on in 1974 and 1975. The block once consisted of similar elegant dwellings, but as the city grew northward, wealthy families sold their properties to commercial developers and moved to newer, more fashionable, quarters uptown. Now the Tredwell House is surrounded by lofts and garages.

Index